A More Christian Industrial Order

A MORE CHRISTIAN INDUSTRIAL ORDER

THE CHRISTIAN'S DUTY
AT WORK AND IN LABOR

HENRY SLOANE COFFIN

THE
Greater Heritage
Christian Publishing
WINTER SPRINGS, FL

A More Christian Industrial Order: The Christian's Duty at Work and in Labor
by Henry Sloane Coffin
Originally published in 1920 as *A More Christian Industrial Order*
by Henry Sloane Coffin
This edition first published March 2023

Published by The Greater Heritage
1170 Tree Swallow Dr., Suite 309
Winter Springs, FL 32708
www.thegreaterheritage.com
info@thegreaterheritage.com

All scripture references are taken from the King James Version (KJV) of the Bible.

Cover Design: The Greater Heritage
Cover Image (paperback and eBook): *Street Scene, Pennsylvania Ave.* (c. 1916-1919). Library of Congress, Prints & Photographs Division, photograph by Harris & Ewing, [LC-DIG-hec-11593].
Cover Image (hardcover): *American Red Cross Hospital Personnel, Lyon, France* (April 1918). Library of Congress, Prints & Photographs Division, American National Red Cross Collection, [LC-DIG-anrc-08154].
Font(s): Fraunces, Mrs Eaves, Sabon LT Pro, Vollkorn.

Printed in the United States of America

Library of Congress Control Number: 2023901277

ISBN (hardcover): 978-1-953855-36-7
ISBN (paperback): 978-1-953855-35-0
ISBN (PDF): 978-1-953855-39-8
ISBN (EPUB): 978-1-953855-37-4

1 2 3 4 5 6 7 8 9 10 27 26 25 24 23

The truest upholders of orderly society are those who set themselves to correct its abuses.

PUBLISHER'S NOTE

This book is a new edition of Henry Sloane Coffin's original book of the same name from 1920. While this non-facsimile version is faithful to its original publication, slight changes have been made to spelling and formatting to place the book in line with modern publishing standards and to make the title easier for contemporary audiences to read. All other aspects of the book have remained unchanged.

CONTENTS

Other Books by Henry Sloane Coffin and
The Greater Heritage...

The Creed of Jesus and Other Sermons

University Sermons

INTRODUCTION

A DISTINGUISHED ethical teacher of New York City recently remarked in conversation: "The Christian Church believes that Jesus is the disclosure of the purpose of God for all time. Why, then, does not the Church find in Jesus a solution for the industrial question of our day and offer the guidance which it claims to possess?" It is a challenge which Christians dare not refuse. It puts to the practical test our assertion that Jesus is the wisdom of God.

There are some who postpone all Christian readjustments of society until the present evil age shall have been ended by the visible advent of Christ in judgment. Until that occurs they see no prospect of abolishing war or terminating industrial strife. But to most Christians of our generation the judgment is no future event merely, but an experience through which we have lived in the awful years of war with its exposure of greed and pride and trust in force. Others are content to sketch the vision of the Christian society as it exists in their ideal; they have no interest in its very partial attainment in the immediate future. But valuable as are such visions to shame the sordid actual and to kindle hope, we who must live in the next five or forty years want guidance for today and tomorrow and the day after.

If by a solution of the industrial question is meant a detailed plan for the organization of the world's work, we know from experience that we cannot expect such explicit guidance from Christ. Our Father shows His confidence in His sons and daughters, and educates us by making us in every century work out the Christian solution for our time. We cannot call our conceptions of what should be, "The Christian Industrial Order." We live in a growing world, and society is a living organism. Nothing final and fixed can be reached in the statement of religious belief or in the formulation of the principles that should govern industry. But we believe that in the Spirit of Jesus we have a Guide enabling us to think out what is our Father's mind for any situation, and we come with that Spirit's leading to the circumstances of our day, and ask what is our Christian duty as producers and consumers, as owners and investors, as employers and employees.

We say that the Spirit of Jesus is our Guide. We are not piecing together Jesus' fragmentary and occasional sayings which have a bearing on industrial matters, and making out of them a law. He and His first followers anticipated in their time a speedy ending of the world. Their relative carelessness of political and economic affairs, and their disparagement of material possessions, are partly accounted for by this expectation. To Paul it did not make much difference whether one were married or unmarried, slave or freeman, in view of the shortness of the time before Christ's return and the beginning of a new age. But allowing for their immediate outlook, and for the political situation in which Christianity came to birth in a subject people in the Roman Empire, there is a Spirit which breathes through the sayings of the Master and of His followers that is applicable to all times, because their interest was not apocalyptic but ethical. To us Christians it is the Spirit of the living God. Each generation is responsible only for its day. We do not blame either our Lord or St. Paul for not attacking the institution of slavery. Emancipation was not a living issue which they had to face. But they faced the issues of their age, and we must face those of ours with their Spirit.

St. Paul pointed out to both the runaway Onesimus and his owner Philemon their Christian obligations. Christianity is not dynamite but leaven. We take the situations in which we find ourselves and seek to permeate them with the mind of Christ. We do not deal with the ideas of democracy as though democracy were the crowning divine arrangement of human history; but democracy is the issue which confronts us today. Our successors, a century or half a century hence, may face other aspects of the problem.

We are not asking what is *the* Christian industrial order, and hoping to see and, if possible, establish the final economic organization of mankind. We are asking what the Spirit of Jesus would create out of the existing social system in order that we may be led into a more Christian industrial order. This is our task assigned us in this our momentous day.

CHAPTER ONE

THE CHRISTIAN AS PRODUCER

IN OUR WORLD where war has wrought such destruction, and want is so widespread, production is the most urgent of problems. Statesmen are summoning their people to work, and every attempt to remedy ills brings us back to the need of more things to be grown and made. And the word "producer" is congenial to the Christian ideal. We are trying to be perfect as our Father is perfect, who is to us the Creator. Every child of His must have a creative occupation. To cultivate the soil to bear food, to drain swamps and increase fruitful acres, to manufacture goods, to train minds, to develop powers of appreciation and add to people's enjoyment, to sharpen consciences to a finer sense of duty, to supply convictions, hopes, reinforcements in God — this is to follow Jesus in becoming like His Father.

This rules out (does it not?) non-productive careers.

If one is not serving the world's comfort or health or knowledge or beauty or faith, he cannot claim the name of Christian. Gentlemen and ladies of leisure, corner loafers and hoboes, whatever their professed religion, are plain pagans. If man or woman is so circumstanced that daily toil is not necessary to keep the wolf from the door, some voluntarily assumed productive labor is a Christian obligation. In a Christianized economic order there will be no leisure class: "If any would not work, neither should he eat" (2 Thess. 3:10). Jewish fathers taught their sons trades, so that Saul, the student destined for the Law, knew how to weave. Ought not some manual labor to be included in all education? And ought not all boys and girls, whatever their families may possess today, be given trades in which they can support themselves and add to the world's wealth? Certainly no one can appropriate the name of the Carpenter of Nazareth and the Teacher of Capernaum, who is not, like Him, augmenting the physical and spiritual goods of mankind.

And this seems to rule out for Christians occupations which do not directly add to human well-being. For some years Church people have eyed with suspicion the business of a distiller or a bartender. They themselves may not have been teetotalers or prohibitionists; but they would not have felt comfortable manufacturing or selling intoxicants, nor did they wish their sons and daughters in this business. Should we not feel similarly towards a number of other callings — towards types of brokerage which do not assist production but help gambling in stocks or cotton or real estate, and towards the work of such middlemen as render no essential service in getting goods from producer to consumer? It may not be possible to legislate these occupations out of existence. It is often difficult to draw sharp lines between callings which do and do not render an essential service. But Christians are men and women of finer conscience than the rest of mankind. We are with God creating a new world by altering the standards of the existing world. We must scrutinize ways of earning a living with the searching mind of Christ, and choose for ourselves, and for boys and girls, callings which are definitely productive. Every Christian is bound to ask: "Is this position of mine a necessary ministry to the family of God's children?" If it be not, we cannot fill it, saying with Jesus: "I must be about my Father's business" (Lk. 2:49).

And as Christians we are opposed to arrangements which prevent men and women from doing the utmost in their callings consistent with their health of mind and body. Christian democracy in industry cannot mean leveling down, retarding the speediest to the pace of the slowest, and limiting the vigorous to the capacities of the frail. That is to restrain God-given powers. In industry, as in other matters, "we then that are strong ought to bear the infirmities of the weak" (Rom. 15:1). There should be fellowship in sharing the results of labor and generous treatment of the less capable but there is nothing Christian in confining the able within the limits of the feeble. The relation of pay to the quantity or quality of work is another matter, and no Christian works primarily for what he makes in money; but every man must be free to give in service to the community as much as in him is.

Christians as producers wish to put *themselves* into their work: "Whatsoever ye do, work heartily," (Col. 3:23) that is "from the soul." The worker's interest and conscience must go into his task, whether that be writing a sermon or feeding a furnace. When so much of the world's work is necessarily mechanical — repeating the same movement of hand or foot thousands of times a day in unison with a machine, sewing buttons on cards, chopping tickets, — it is not easy to let the result express the laborer's self.

And in so many industries the individual worker is one of a vast army, doing again and again a single small part in a complicated process, that it is hard for him to see that he is embodying himself in the product. It seems essential for the preservation and development of his personality, for the enlistment of his soul, that he have some voice in the conduct of the enterprise. To a degree this is true already where labor is organized; but its voice speaks rarely save to protest or threaten, and there is scanty opportunity for its speaking productively. Politically we are trying a form of government which expresses our collective selves. "We, the people of the United States," our *Constitution* commences.

Our government had its people behind it in the war, not only because the leaders were of our choosing, but also because they had so to lead as to carry public opinion with them. "War," we were repeatedly told, "is dependent upon the *morale* of the entire population." Production is similarly a matter of the spirit of all the participants in an industry. Should not the leaders in a business hold their positions as representatives of the investors and workers in that undertaking? Should not the enterprise be so organized that it is responsive to and expressive of the minds and consciences of all engaged in it? That would mean that its affairs were made known to and shared in by all concerned in it. Democracy is not mainly a matter of voting, although some means of registering opinion and exercising control, have to be devised; it is more a matter of a fellowship of spirit. A church has to be led by ministers and officers who command the sympathy and utter the ideals of the congregation. As a rule a mere fraction of the people take part in the annual meeting; but all the while leaders feel out the will of the led and keep their backing. Must there not be in a store or a factory a similar fellowship — the sense that the leaders represent the workers and that every person involved in the business is given the chance to express himself in it? Until the humblest laborer says instinctively, "*we,* in *our* business," there is not the *morale* for production.

And this democratic readjustment of industry is of vital interest to us as Christians. We are trying to produce self-reliant and brotherly sons of God. The present organization of society often thwarts us and actually undoes our work. A Scotch missionary in India, speaking of the political situation there, wrote recently:

> Those who have been engaged in the work of missionary colleges in India must have been struck by the tendency of young men who, in their student days, had come very near to the Kingdom, to revert with years to a more Hindu type of faith. It is my belief that the cause is partly this: that under the influence of Christian education they had been inspired with very Christian dreams of a life of free and noble service, but finding no career open to them of the kind for which they had hoped, they gradually acquired that mood of disillusionment and world-weariness to which philosophical Hinduism especially appeals. If

> this be at all a true diagnosis of the case, may not the gradual introduction of the institutions of responsible government, with the careers of public usefulness which that would throw open, prove to be just the supplement which missionary education requires for its abiding and widespread fruitfulness?

And that can be said of our own business world. In home and school and church a young Christian is inspired to "a life of free and noble service." He enters an office or a factory where service of the community is not the pervading motive, but the making of profits. If without capital, he has no sense of proprietorship in the business, and consequently feels scant responsibility for its efficiency. So long as he receives his wages, he has no zeal in piling up the profits of the proprietors of the concern. Or if he be a large stockholder, he finds a gulf between himself and the mass of the workers; he is not responsible to them, and in many instances he feels that their interests are antagonistic to his. He usually has little personal contact with them, and loses the sense of comradeship in toil. The want of self-expression and the want of fellowship destroy Christian character and impoverish both factors in our industrial enterprises. Men acquire the mood of disillusionment and become, if not Hindus, cynics and pessimists.

Our Christian interest is not first in the distribution of the gains of industry as wages or dividends. Increasing pay does not necessarily procure better work, nor do larger wages or profits mean better men. Most of the finest work in the world can never be paid for, and we shall not solve our industrial difficulties by treating them as questions of money. Strikes settled by granting higher pay seldom stay settled. We are concerned with the *status* of workers and investors as sons and daughters of God. We wish them all to have the chance to put their consciences into industry, and to work together in it as a company of Christian brethren. Maximum production results from a right spiritual adjustment of those who labor. It is plain that men's hearts are not in the enterprises of today; and the consequent production is often half, or considerably less than half, what it might be. Must we not look for solutions that will give men a feeling of proprietorship and obligation in their work, a voice in its control and a knowledge of its policies, with an appeal in it to their hearts to do their utmost for the service of the community?

Fundamentally we Christians are interested in producing sons and daughters of God after the likeness of Christ, confident that such workers will produce the requisite goods for men's bodies and minds. We, therefore, scan our industries as formers of character. What sort of persons does this department store, or this railroad, or this domestic employment, make of those who engage in its work? Many will deny that man-making is the business of factories and mines and offices; they will assign that function to the home, the school, and the church. "We are mining coal not men; we are producing shirt-waists, not women; we are transporting freight, not carrying workmen from one moral level to another." And to be sure home and school and church have an earlier and a bigger chance to mold character; but our industries and professions, whether they acknowledge the obligation or not, are in the man-making trade. Shakespeare was right when he spoke of his nature as "subdued to what it works in, like the dyer's hand." A physician's, or an insurance agent's, or a banker's, or a butler's, occupation usually sets its distinctive mark on him. He has the air of his calling.

There is a subtle atmosphere about a store or an office which infects those who work there. If services are rewarded by tips, a premium is placed on servility. If competitors are to be outwitted, shrewd trickery is encouraged. The conditions of a calling shape the men and women in it. As producers of Christlike children of God, we cannot be indifferent to these man-making or man-marring circumstances in occupations. Each of us has to ask what sort of persons does the household of which we are part, or the business undertaking in which we gain our living, create?

It is evident that the problem of production is of the utmost seriousness at the moment. Every strike or lockout decreases the supply of something which men need, sends up prices, entails suffering, and worst of all breeds bitterness. The will to work is not in the mass of mankind. What is wanted is an infusion of the creative spirit, and that is the task of religion, for the creative spirit is the Spirit of God.

Religion kindles the imagination. Once let a man have God in his mind, let him look out on the world and see God's hands everywhere shaping mountain and seashore, plant and human form, eye for beauty and heart to love, and he will connect his work with the business of the Most High. He is building a house for men to dwell in, or meeting their need for food, or furnishing access to knowledge. Vision is the incentive to labor. In the war we sought to have soldiers and sailors *see* for what they were enduring and toiling and hazarding their all. It was a vision of a free and fraternal world that caught the devotion of the finest spirits. Too few people see mankind's necessities of body, mind and soul, and view their tasks as answers to them. Faith supplies the vision of God, and brings men to say: "My Father worketh hitherto, and I work" (Jn. 5:17).

Religion furnishes an adequate motive to make a man do his best. Personal ambition is a strong incentive, but in many occupations there is no getting ahead, and by middle age most men have little advancement in prospect. Self-interest drives some people a long distance, but it does not move the best persons, nor appeal to the highest in any of us, and after a certain point it has no power to keep at work those who think themselves comfortable. Love of one's family and the desire to do for them is a more compelling motive, and it has kinship with the highest. But only devotion to an ideal, a feeling of obligation to the family of God, will send men day after day to their labor with consecration of heart and soul. That is faith's contribution to industry: "Here are your brethren in the household of God. Here are you with God-given strength and skill. Here is your Father serving His children, serving you, and counting on you to serve with Him." And the believing toiler responds, declaring as he pounds a typewriter or wields a pick: "We are God's fellow-workers."

And religion sets men in fellowship with one another. No believer in the Father of Jesus Christ, be he an unskilled laborer or a many-millioned capitalist, can be content to find himself separated from fellow children of God by hostile class-interest. If he be among the less privileged, it is not surprising that he should look out upon the world today with a sense of injustice, and not for himself alone, but for millions of his kind deprived of the chance of full lives in things true, lovely and honorable, and should resolve to assert the right of the lowliest workers to a voice in the control of the industries in which they toil.

If he be among the more privileged, it would be shocking if he should take it for granted that he was entitled to a so much larger share of earth's advantages than his brethren enjoy, if he should attempt to keep them in their present place and himself in his, and have no sympathy with those who are trying to compass a more fraternal organization of our business enterprises, and if he should not welcome the chance to be brought into closer community of interest with the mass of his fellow-mortals. His religion may not tell him precisely how this closer fellowship is to be worked out in the trade or craft with which he is concerned. But if it be genuinely Christian religion, it will make him open-minded to inquire into all fraternal methods of industrial readjustment, and very ready, even at personal sacrifice, to remove causes of envy, misunderstanding and ill will.

For it is fellowship which enables men to compass their finest achievements. When the carpenter encourages the goldsmith, when the captain and the lieutenant and the private of industry understand and trust each other, when the whole force in an enterprise pulls together, there is Christian production — the animating Holy Spirit of brotherhood. Then there will be produced sufficient goods, and — better still — Christian men and women.

CHAPTER TWO

THE CHRISTIAN AS CONSUMER

THE WORD "consumer," unlike the word "producer," does not at once connect itself in our thought with the Christian point of view. It suggests "using up," and fills us with alarm. But the underlying faith of the entire Bible is that the Lord of the universe is a bountiful Father, who provides in no niggardly fashion for His children's necessities. In His house, as Jesus pictured it in a parable, there is "enough and to spare" for the entire household. A psalmist sings: "Thou openest thine hand, and satisfiest the desire of every living thing. The Lord is righteous in all his ways, and holy in all his works" (Ps. 145:16-17). The dismal forebodings of those who predict a famine-stricken world, where population exceeds the supply of food, are at variance with the confidence of Jewish and Christian believers. Such apprehensions cast a serious reflection upon the housekeeping abilities of our

Father God. Israelites, whose country was vastly poorer than many other parts of the globe, spoke of it as a land flowing with milk and honey.

> And of Joseph he said, Blessed of the Lord be his land, for the precious things of heaven, for the dew, and for the deep that coucheth beneath, And for the precious fruits brought forth by the sun, and for the precious things put forth by the moon, And for the chief things of the ancient mountains, and for the precious things of the lasting hills, And for the precious things of the earth and fulness thereof. (Deuteronomy 33:13-15)

That is an ancient and poetical way of expressing the assumption of present-day scientists that there are incalculable resources of heat, of force, of productivity, in atmosphere and soil, awaiting discovery. Every investigator in chemistry, in physics, in medicine and agriculture, takes it for granted that new factors for healing or power or fertility are latent, and can be found and utilized. It is the unconscious testimony of the human heart to its trust in a faithful Creator. If there be a shortage of a staple commodity, if there be a human being in physical want, it is not God's will, but the result of man's ignorant or foolish or unjust management. God may use poverty, as He employs every circumstance, for our education; but He never chooses it of preference; it is forced upon Him by our blunders. It may be the consequence of an individual's recklessness or laziness. It may be due to the wicked destruction of war — and war is never God's method of settling differences, but a desperate last resort when we have disregarded His ways. Poverty is oftener to be set down to the unbrotherly social conscience which in the midst of God's plenty allows some of His children to be born disinherited, to grow up unendowed, to labor insufficiently rewarded, to become ill or old or uncared for. Our Father is Himself open-handed; the pinch of penury comes from the slothful or grasping hand of man.

Hence there is nothing religious in abstemiousness. "The Son of man came eating and drinking" (Matt. 11:19). He was called by His critics "a gluttonous man and a winebibber" (Matt. 11:19). Food for body, for eye, for mind, for heart, for soul, is here to be taken. "For every creature of God is good, and nothing to be refused, if it be received with thanksgiving" (1 Tim. 4:4). The only kind of fasting which is thoroughly Christian is that wise self-control which orders diet so as to keep one's self entirely fit for God's service. There is no virtue in self-denial, nothing meritorious in refraining from things pleasant. There may be self-denial for the sake of others, but Christ's purpose for us is life abundant. Some Christians have felt that things agreeable were dangerous. Lady Stephen once asked her son: "Did you ever know your father do a thing because it was pleasant?" And Sir Leslie Stephen says that his father once smoked a cigar but found it so delicious that he never smoked again. There are excellent reasons to be found for not smoking, but certainly not this. God "giveth us richly all things to enjoy" (1 Tim. 6:17). Our capacities of appreciation are measures of our Christlikeness.

But while our Father is open-handed. He does not allow waste. In the story of the manna, every man is said to take according to his need: "he that gathered much had nothing over, and he that gathered little had no lack" (Exo. 16:18). Jesus was at pains to instill in His disciples the lesson of thrift. He made them go about after the crowds had been fed, and collect in baskets the broken pieces that remained. Food was to Him too precious as a means of life to allow it to be squandered. The small boy who breaks an empty milk-bottle on the street for the sheer fun of smashing something and unconsciously increases the expenses of the milk industry, the follower of fashion who discards clothing before it is outworn in order to keep up with the arbitrarily set "latest style," the person who takes more on his plate than he eats, the lumber company which denudes a mountain-side without providing for a future growth, the wholesalers who allow a cargo of fish to rot rather than suffer prices to be lowered, the farmers who throw away part of a crop to keep up the market — every waster in the community is to that extent antichristian. War-time economics in food, in clothes, in fuel, in labor, were an admirable discipline for this extravagant people. A follower of Jesus is one who puts everything which he is and has to fullest use.

And our Father's bounty places on the family the obligation of seeing that His generous supplies are wisely and fairly distributed. Ought any to have cake, while some lack bread? When nations felt the necessity of keeping their people united in order to win a war, they did not trust the hit-and-miss methods of individual initiative, and the "natural laws" of demand and supply, so loudly commended by economists of a bygone generation; but they made it a public concern to see that no inhabitant of the land was in needless want. Is the maintenance of national unity and goodwill any less essential in peace to prevent class conflicts and to enable a people fully to discharge its duties to mankind? Why, then, do away with our public controls? We tried collective housekeeping on a national scale. There were priority lists in fuel, which made it impossible for a man of wealth to consume coal in running a greenhouse, while many homes or workrooms went un-heated. Patriotic pressure prevented the devotion of soil, labor and fertilizer to lawns and flower-beds, when there was danger of insufficient wheat and potatoes. Our world would be the poorer were there no orchids or chrysanthemums; and it seems plain that a Creator who makes possible the lovely does not wish it uncultivated. But is it Christian that a community should allow any of its school-children to be underfed, or any of its workers to be un-healthily housed, while some of its people indulge themselves in lavish outlays for personal pleasure? Granting that many well-to-do persons are prepared to contribute their share to relieve poverty, it is patent that many others are not, and that private initiative in the form of charity, however well-organized, is inadequate. Can a city be called Christian, can it be called Old Testament Jewish, which permits children to grow up physically unfit, as our draft-boards found numbers of young men, and which herds together in overcrowded blocks not idle paupers but thousands of its hardest-working laboring people who perform most of its disagreeable and straining chores, while a portion of its inhabitants are allowed to spend huge sums on various amusements, or on personal adornment, or on the gratification of their whims and fancies?

It is easy to point out that the kind of city government to which we Americans are accustomed to treat ourselves, with occasional intervals of political sanity, is ill-fitted to handle these economic questions, and would handle them extravagantly and possibly corruptly. But we have the kind of government which we deserve, and we can have a better any time we make up our minds to take the necessary trouble. A government with more social obligations would enlist the interest and service of the socially minded. Nor is it desirable that many of these social tasks, like the feeding of under-nourished children, should be a function of either government or of private charity; feeding is a responsibility of the family. Such wages as will support a man and his dependents in reasonable comfort ought to be a first charge upon every industry. This has been one of the laudable aims of organized labor. It probably will be a necessary duty of government to see that every willing worker is offered employment, and to keep some public work in reserve for slack periods.

The main point for us to stress is that luxury and want cannot exist side by side in any community which calls itself Christian. This is not to say that inequalities in possessions are unchristian. So long as God gives us five-talent and two-talent and one-talent men and women, there will be differences in wealth. But while a community has sufficient food, no child can be allowed the physical handicap of under-nourishment, any more than we tolerate his remaining illiterate. As a community we must determine a minimum standard of living, and consider it a public obligation to see that no family lacks the chance to earn that.

Doubtless this involves some form of public control of essential industries. We cannot trust the self-interest either of leaders or of laborers to achieve the result; there must be some authoritative representative of the community whom both serve and to whom both are accountable. Nor can we rely on so-called "natural laws," like that of supply and demand, to meet our economic needs. No farmer trusts natural laws to produce a crop; he cultivates the soil. "Nature," whether in a field or a human group is responsive to intelligent stimuli. Social relations are to be made productive, as we till a field. Children of God are not meant to take anxious thought, saying, "What shall we eat? or, What shall we drink? or, Wherewithal shall we be clothed?" (Matt. 6:31). Our thought is to have other interests; and our Father, who knows that we have need of these things, abundantly provides the requisite supply, especially in this richly favored country (Matt. 6:32). But unless we make it a family concern to see that a wise and just distribution is assured, a great many sons and daughters of God are doomed to take unchristian anxious thought. Some may say that fear of want is the only sufficient antidote to laziness, the only goad which will drive men to work. That is true in some cases, and we shall have to conserve wholesome compulsions against idleness. Paul had no pity upon loafers among the Thessalonians. But fear of want is hardly a Christian motive to be encouraged. Fear never produces the best work, as slavery attests. When men are freed from fear, they can concentrate on good workmanship. And "give us this day our daily bread" (Matt. 6:11) is a social prayer, carrying with it a collective responsibility so to employ God's liberal answer that none is overlooked.

If the hastily improvised attempts at public control during the war were not altogether satisfactory, that is not surprising. In this country from the earliest days we have cultivated private enterprise, and we are still novices at teamwork. Our various war boards accomplished some excellent results in bettering the *status* of labor, in eliminating speculative middlemen, in distributing the supplies where they were needed, and occasionally in lowering costs of production. Our mistakes are no reason for giving up the attempt to learn to operate an industrial commonwealth, democratically controlled, in which, however the machinery be organized, want, save as the result of sloth or of wrongdoing, is unknown.

And as Christians we cannot limit this fellowship of consumers by national boundaries. When, immediately after the Armistice, a few ministers ventured to say from their pulpits that it was a Christian duty to restore former enemies to fellowship and to meet their urgent needs for food, for credit, for raw materials, they were instantly challenged by irate patriots; but just one year later leading American bankers and businessmen made a public plea for the assistance of Germany's industrial recuperation as the only means of saving her from Bolshevism.

When will we learn that our Christian instincts are our safest guides in practical affairs, and that "the foolishness of God is wiser than men?" (1 Cor. 1:25). The "us" and "our" of the Lord's prayer include mankind. Nations are to serve each other in commerce and industry, and missionary motives must control both. The international labor conferences provided for in the Covenant of the League of Nations are happy signs of the growth of a Christian conscience in the world. Pauper conditions in China and India are the concern of America. A minimum standard of decently comfortable living there is necessary to safeguard the standards here, not to speak of what we owe our needy brother and his dependents yonder, exactly as we are responsible for some needy family only a block away. As we learn commercial foreign missions we shall hear less from provincial souls who wish to furnish the bread of life to limited districts only, and to suffer the more remote to stay their spirits on any starvation diet available. We may hope that our war experiences in sharing food and fuel with our allies, and our present experiences of extending credit to former enemies, will form in us a fraternal conscience that shall govern us in future trade and tariff discussions, and dominate our spirit in our rapidly expanding foreign commerce. As consumers we must cultivate the sense of membership in an earth-wide household of God.

While we accept all good things at the hand of a generous Providence, we cannot forget that almost none of them reach us without the toil of human hands. What we consume is in part the labor of men and women. We must inquire what it is which we eat and drink, and with what we are clothed and amused. David once longed for a drink from the well of his native Bethlehem, and three of his bold followers gratified his wish by breaking through the Philistine lines at the risk of their lives and fetching him water. But David "would not drink thereof. And he said, Be it far from me, O Lord, that I should do this: is not this the blood of the men that went in jeopardy of their lives?" (2 Sam. 23:16-17).

Like him, we surely will refuse to consume the school hours and playtime and future health of children, doomed by poverty or greed of parents to premature toil; or to drain the motherly attention of women taken out of their homes to factories and offices, when they should be bringing up their little ones; or to eat the leisure of men for rest and worship and family-life, who are denied a weekly rest-day and are kept overlong at toil. Hood's *Song of the Shirt* is sadly still applicable to some workers in our cities:

"Work—work—work,
Till the brain begins to swim;
Work—work—work,
Till the eyes are heavy and dim!
Seam, and gusset, and band,
Band, and gusset, and seam,
Till over the buttons I fall asleep,
And sew them on in a dream!

"O, men, with sisters dear!
O, men, with mothers and wives!
It is not linen you're wearing out,
But human creatures' lives!
Stitch—stitch—stitch,
In poverty, hunger and dirt,
Sewing at once, with a double thread,
A Shroud as well as a Shirt.

We cannot have our necessities met by industries in which the operatives jeopardize their health or their safety; and we recall that the casualties of our mines, factories and railways are annually in excess of our losses in the war. It is not pleasant reading to look over the figures of occupational diseases, or to scan the statistics of the length of life in certain callings. A modem David would pause before using the products of some of our industries: there is much more blood on them than we realize. In the stoke-room on ocean liners, in the furnaces of steel plants, in glass factories, on fishing smacks off our coast in winter, beneath the rivers where "sand-hogs" sink tunnels for our transit lines, hardships and dangers are encountered comparable to those faced by our soldiers and sailors, and with none of the patriotic attention which was paid them. And some of the world's work is necessarily wearing drudgery or extremely repugnant. Should we not recognize the principle that the more disagreeable a calling is, like handling garbage or working in the humid atmosphere of a tobacco factory or in the extreme heat of a furnace, and the more straining on nerves or dulling to intelligence, the shorter the period of employment should be? And there are forms of some occupations, now tolerated, like certain theatrical performances, in which spectators consume the modesty and self-respect of young women. Shall we amuse ourselves at the price of blood?

No American can have read with satisfaction the reports submitted as a working basis for the first International Labor Conference in Washington. Sixteen countries have eight-hour laws applicable to most industries, but ours is not on that list. Twenty-one lands place special safeguards about the employment of mothers before and after childbirth, but ours is not recorded among them. Nearly every industrial nation forbids the employment in factories of children under fourteen, but Romania, India, Spain, China, *and the United States of America* (what company to be in!) are among the lands not yet on that ethical level. When we speak of Americanizing our foreign-born population, to what are we lifting them?

As individuals, we cannot, like David, know just what it is that we consume. As members of a yet unchristianized community, we may well beware of blood, and demand public supervision, both in our own and other lands, of the conditions under which the world's work is done, and the enactment of safeguards for the lives of our comrades in the fellowship of labor.

To the Corinthian Christians St. Paul wrote: "When ye come together therefore into one place, this is not to eat the Lord's supper. For in eating every one taketh before other his own supper: and one is hungry, and another is drunken" (1 Cor. 11:20-21). The grasping and competitive spirit of Corinth had invaded the fellowship of the Church, and the love-feast had become a disorderly grab, where one overdrank while another found nothing left for him. Our Lord often likened His kingdom to a feast. Life seemed to Him a festive banquet, spread by a generous Father. The whole of it should be sacramental — suggestive of God's continual presence with us, His loving and thoughtful care unfailingly given to every one of His children. Instead of letting the spirit of Corinth invade the fellowship of the Church, it is our task as Christians to carry the spirit of the Lord's Table — our thankfulness to the Provider of all good, our considerate thought that all our brethren in Christ share with us, our own care that we use aright what we ourselves receive — into the Corinths where we dwell, and so employ the gifts of God in food and drink, in fuel and clothing, in comforts and delights, in knowledge and inspirations, that all life becomes as suggestive of God as the Supper of the Lord Jesus Christ.

CHAPTER THREE

THE CHRISTIAN AS OWNER

THE FUNDAMENTAL PRINCIPLE of the Bible regarding property is that God is the owner of everything. David, speaking of Israel's offerings for the building of the Temple, is reported by the Chronicler as praying:

> Thine, O Lord is the greatness, and the power, and the glory, and the victory, and the majesty: for all that is in the heaven and in the earth is thine; thine is the kingdom, O Lord, and thou art exalted as head above all. Both riches and honour come of thee, and thou reignest over all; and in thine hand is power and might; and in thine hand it is to make great, and to give strength unto all. Now therefore, our God, we thank thee, and praise thy glorious name. But who am I, and what is my people, that we should

> be able to offer so willingly after this sort? for all things come of thee, and of thine own have we given thee. For we are strangers before thee, and sojourners, as were all our fathers: our days on the earth are as a shadow, and there is none abiding. O Lord our God, all this store that we have prepared to build thee an house for thine holy name cometh of thine hand, and is all thine own. I know also, my God, that thou triest the heart, and hast pleasure in uprightness. As for me, in the uprightness of mine heart I have willingly offered all these things: and now have I seen with joy thy people, which are present here, to offer willingly unto thee. O Lord God of Abraham, Isaac, and of Israel, our fathers, keep this for ever in the imagination of the thoughts of the heart of thy people, and prepare their heart unto thee. (1 Chronicles 29:11-18)

Man's tenure of anything can be only for a few years: "for" runs this same prayer, "we are strangers before thee, and sojourners, as were all our fathers: our days on the earth are as a shadow, and there is none abiding" (1 Chron. 29:15). All that men possess is a loan terminable at the will of the Divine Lender: "For we brought nothing into this world, and it is certain we can carry nothing out"

(1 Tim. 6:7). Property belongs to God, and remains in His disposal. When friends and family were gone. Job said: "The Lord gave, and the Lord hath taken away," (Job 1:21). As human beings, therefore, we have no property rights. No man may say: "Is it not lawful for me to do what I will with mine own?" (Matt. 20:15). The Divine Voice challenges him: "What hast thou that thou didst not receive?" (1 Cor. 4:7) and he must be prepared to give to the real Owner an account of his stewardship.

The second principle is that God loans possessions to the community of His children, and to individuals through the community. In the Old Testament the community is the nation. The land belongs to Israel, and is allotted among its tribes and families. According to the ideal of *Leviticus* it "shall not be sold for ever," (Lev. 25:23) but shall revert in the jubilee year to its original owner. The prophets in an age of industrial change, when a wealthy class was rising and becoming possessors of the land, while a dependent class tilled it, constantly denounced this state of things as an infraction of brotherhood:

> The Lord will enter into judgment with the ancients of his people, and the princes thereof: for ye have eaten up the vineyard; the spoil of the poor is in your houses. What mean ye that ye beat my people to pieces, and grind the faces

> of the poor? saith the Lord God of hosts. (Isaiah 3:14-15)

And,

> Woe unto them that join house to house, that lay field to field, till there be no place, that they may be placed alone in the midst of the earth! (Isaiah 5:8)

After the Exile, Nehemiah persuades the well-to-do to restore to every Israelite his small ancestral holding, so that none is without a home and the means of earning his living.

In the New Testament the community is the whole family of mankind; and the Church, which considers herself bound to exemplify what the world should become, attempts in Jerusalem a common holding of possessions, so that no believer is allowed to want, and wealthier Christians place their property at the call of the brotherhood. This is hardly an industrial system. It seems to have been instituted only in Jerusalem, and then probably because of poverty. It was not compulsory upon Christians, for Peter says to Ananias of his property: "Whiles it remained, was it not thine own? and after it was sold, was it not in thine own power?" (Acts

5:4). It was a fraternal attempt under high emotion to create a common store for the community's needs. As an economic experiment it was not a success, for we find Paul constantly taking up a collection for the poor Christians at Jerusalem in all his churches, where no such communistic plan was attempted. But the underlying principle is clear that Christians regarded property as God's loan to the community of His believing children. In our circumstances this would be interpreted to stress the social control of property.

And third, the Bible implies that it is the community's duty to see that every member of society is a property-owner. So far from minimizing the moral worth of possessions, the Bible considers ownership of property most valuable for the development of character. When St. Paul is trying to make a man out of a thief, he writes: "let him labour...that he may *have*" (Eph. 4:28, emphasis mine). Until the man possesses something which he calls his own, he is hardly a complete man, and therefore he will lack a sense of social obligation and be unable to feel himself a full member of society. Paul shows him what to do with his possessions: "that he may have to give to him that needeth" (Eph. 4:28). But he cannot *give* until he *has*. That which a man controls extends his personality and exercises his conscience. Public spirit is unlikely to be found in those who own nothing. Patriotism comes with a stake in the country. Since for Christians the main business of life is to grow a brotherly conscience, property is a great spiritual asset. In the picture of the early Church in the Book of the Acts, it is written: "neither said any of them that ought of the things which he possessed was his own" (Acts 4:32) but the "say" was his, and in the voluntary placing of his possessions at the command of the fellowship, each disciple used his conscience.

A Christian's main quarrel with the existing economic order is not that some possess large wealth, but that so many possess practically nothing. A big fortune is a perilous trust, but a Christian may be trained to administer it conscientiously; and we have known men and women of large means who probably made their money do more good for the community than a numerous group of small owners might have done with a similar amount. When, however, a man is without property, it is difficult today to educate him in a Christian sense of obligation. Indeed the Christian appeal seems not as likely to awaken response in the possessionless, as in those who own something. Farmers, and even tenant-farmers, are more apt to connect themselves with a church than are the farm laborers. The property-less are restless. They do not consider that the community does much for them, and they do not feel bound to do aught for it. The I. W. W. (Industrial Workers of the World) and similar extreme radicals are recruited from the workers in mines, lumber-camps, and factories, who have nothing of their own. They lack a feeling of responsibility for the country, or for the town in which they live; and it is to consciences awake that the Christian Gospel mainly appeals. Our reshaping of society will not be directed towards taking wealth away from its possessors, but towards giving those with nothing the chance to call something their own. Property is an enlargement of personality; and ownership is a spiritual relation which we crave for every child of God.

To be sure we cannot pass over the constantly repeated warnings in the New Testament, and especially from the lips of our Lord Himself, of the dangers of wealth.

> And Jesus looked round about, and saith unto his disciples, How hardly shall they that have riches enter into the kingdom of God! And the disciples were astonished at his words. But Jesus answereth again, and saith unto them, Children, how hard is it for them that trust in riches to enter into the kingdom of God! It is easier for a camel to go through the eye of a needle, than for a rich man to enter into the kingdom of God. (Mark 10:23-25)

Very few wealthy persons are not cumbered by their

possessions and hindered from personal human service. Inasmuch as they feel themselves expected to live upon a certain scale and to do as others of their position do, they have houses and estates which require the labor of many to keep up and which increase their cares; and the maintenance of their possessions engrosses their time and thought. Rarely do rich men or women take active part in civic and religious organizations; their belongings hamper their personal activity. Riches tend to place their possessors in a suspicious attitude towards people; there are so many hangers-on to take advantage of them; they become wary, distrustful, and often inhumanly isolated. Riches tend to render them self-sufficient, self-important, self-indulgent. No wonder Jesus found them hostile to the childlike spirit which the kingdom demands.

Religious leaders have either, like Francis of Assisi, espoused poverty, or at least looked askance at large fortunes. Martin Luther wrote to his friend, Spalatin: "It is said that Schifer is dead, and has left a million gulden to Dr. Carola. He would indeed be a bold Christian who would not dread such a mountain of gold." We have all known some men and women of large means who were conspicuously hard-working, fraternal, humble, self-spending disciples of Christ. They seemed successfully to be passing through the needle's eye, and none could dispute their useful place in the kingdom of God. Further it is fair to admit that in our country and time it seems hard for those without property to enter the kingdom, perhaps fully as hard as for those with many millions. Both for spiritual development and for vigorous personal service, an industrial order is desirable which attempts to answer Agur's wise prayer: "Give me neither poverty nor riches" (Prov. 30:8).

An eminent British economist, Professor Hobhouse of London University, has drawn a suggestive distinction between two kinds of property, which he terms, "property for use" and "property for power." By the former he means these possessions which a man uses for himself in association with his nearest and dearest — a house, a garden, tools or equipment for his work. By the latter his share in and control of industrial enterprises which make him master of other lives. He points out that there is a difference between the possession of things which gives a man freedom and security, and the control of other persons through things, which gives power. He argues that the first should be secured to the individual as private property, while the second should be kept under the scrutiny and control of the democratic state. The clear working out of the distinction is no easy matter; but it suggests a clew to what is mainly the individual's and what is mainly society's part in the ownership of property.

Our first concern as Christians today is that every

man shall have the chance to become an owner. Israel's national history began in a labor movement by people who felt that as slaves without possessions of their own they could not be truly religious: "And the Lord spake unto Moses, Go unto Pharaoh, and say unto him, Thus saith the Lord, Let my people go, that they may serve me" (Exo. 8:1). If a man is a bondman whose work and idleness are not in his own power, whose conscience cannot control his labor, who is without stimuli to initiative, to perseverance, to thrift, to generosity, he is handicapped in attaining sonship with God. Israel, born into national life in this struggle for industrial liberty, carefully protected a man's chance to work and his possession of tools. "No man shall take the mill or the upper mill-stone to pledge; for he taketh a man's life to pledge" (Deut. 24:6). That with which a man earns his living for himself and his family, and renders his service to the community, ought to be sacredly conserved to him. He should own at least that — the means to support his dependents in reasonable comfort.

It becomes difficult to interpret this in our more complex modern society, where many persons are not land-owners and where most of the world's work is done by machinery. An acre or two of soil and a couple of mill-stones are a simple problem beside a laborer's rights to be housed and to a *status* in the mine where he picks coal, or the plant in which he pours steel, or the many-acred farm on which he is one of a gang running tractor plows and huge reapers and binders. It is even more difficult to think through the question of the *status* of employees in department stores, railways, offices, households. What is the present day equivalent of the small holding of land and the mill? This must be patiently thought out by those with first-hand acquaintance with particular industries and with commercial enterprises. But the Biblical ideal seems to demand under modern conditions that a worker be assured a stake in the enterprise in which he labors, so that he has a reasonable security of employment at a return which will keep him and his family at a standard which the community regards as just.

Our next concern as Christians is the establishment of the principle that property exists for people, and not people for property. Possessions are excellent servants but ruinous masters. "Take heed, and beware of covetousness: for a man's life consisteth not in the abundance of the things which he possesseth" (Lk. 12:15). This was a saying spoken to a man with a desire for a larger share of an estate. It applies both to those who have wealth and to those who would like to have it. When a Christian finds that the care of his property so engrosses him that he is prevented from giving his community his personal service, Christ would urge him, as He did the rich young ruler, to disembarrass himself of the impeding possessions. It is our personal relations with men that count for both them and ourselves. If a man has so many houses or places to keep up, or feels that his private interests so absorb his whole energy, that he cannot take on civic and church responsibilities, a Christian apostle would bid him "lay aside" part at least of this "weight" (Heb. 12:1). It would be better for him to be poorer in goods and wealthier in contacts with men and women. If a woman feels that her occupation with the domestic and financial problem of living upon a certain scale, hinders her from using fully her abilities for human helpfulness, Jesus would certainly deal with her, as He dealt with Martha, and warn her that she was missing "the good part" (Lk. 10:41-42). And we may be sure that He would be equally frank with that large number of poorer persons who are always thinking of money, and of what money could buy, and wishing they had it.

In a community properly rights must never be allowed to stand in the way of human well-being. Time and again the defenders of certain interests — the race-track proprietors when gambling was under discussion, the brewers and saloon-keepers when prohibition is to the fore, manufacturers and mine-owners when legislation to prevent overlong hours or the employment of women and children, or to compel appliances against accidents, is up, owners of buildings and real estate interests when sanitary or fire laws are in point, plead the rights of property in opposition to those who argue for human lives. To be sure some reformers are unwise, and no man whose business has been held legitimate ought to be unfairly dealt with by a sudden change of law. But a Christian community cannot measure its wealth by the profits of its industries or the volume of its trade, but by the richness of the lives of its men, women and children. A city's worth must be computed in terms of the characters and services of its citizens. Like the Sabbath, things are for folks, not folks for things.

Our supreme interests with property is that men should hold whatever they own as a trust allotted to them by their Father God through the community of His children. No man can possess anything more than his own brute strength may seize and keep save as society by its customs, laws, and police, assures him in his property. He must, therefore, use it as their trustee under God. Whatever we spend upon our own or our family's housing, clothing, food, amusement, comfort, must be viewed as a public allowance to us. We must mentally open our books to the eyes of the brotherhood of our fellow-citizens and of the world-wide family of God, and show them: "Thus and thus, have I done with that which was yours and mine." They naturally ask themselves whether we and our families are worth our keep, whether our services to the city, the country, the world, are commensurate with the outlay made upon us. No self-respecting man wishes to be carried by the community; he wants to pay his way. Whatever any one employs to maintain himself and his dependents, whether it comes as income from an inheritance or from an investment of his savings, from the earnings of a business in which he shares or from his wages, is a salary which the human race pays him. As Christians we wish to be honest, and render an equivalent in work of mind and heart and hand. At the bar of our consciences we must make up our accounts with the family of God's children, and be answerable to them.

Such an accounting is no light thing. Men used to tremble in anticipation of the Day of Judgment, and wonder how their reckoning would stand. We no longer think of a dramatic scene in the presence of the returning Christ and His angels. The judgement is for us a continuous process, and it is going on now. The books are kept in our own characters and in our influence for good or ill upon our neighbors, and kept with an accuracy which rivals that of any recording angel. Christ is for us constantly arriving; His kingdom is always at hand; and His Spirit is waiting to dominate all hearts and all spheres of human life. The eyes, of which we think as scanning our records, are not those only of the Son of man who looks to see how we deal with the least of His brethren, but also those of our brethren themselves, small and great, — recent comers to our city, a child born last night, boys and girls, men and women, of every land — all peering over the pages of our accounting of that which is theirs as well as ours. Are we square with society? We have "property for use;" can we satisfy our brethren, can we satisfy our consciences before them, that we are employing it wisely and faithfully? Some of us have "property for power:" we control, or control in part, the conditions under which they labor. Can we face them, and face our consciences in their presence? Surely these are queries as searching as any which our conscientious forefathers proposed to themselves in their self-examinations preparatory to the final judgment. And they are questions which we are not left free today to put or not as we choose; they are being forced upon us by the spirit of our time, by men and women awake to social obligations, by young men who were told that they owed their country and humanity their lives and must not withhold them in a day of need, and who are insistent that each owner of property be told the service which he owes country and world. A judgment day is here, and every one of us must be fully prepared to give an account of his stewardship at the bar of the social conscience.

To Christians ownership of property is a momentous

matter, for, like kinship with people, it seems an abiding spiritual relation. In a striking passage Jesus places our relations to things and to people side by side:

> And Jesus answered and said, Verily I say unto you, There is no man that hath left house, or brethren, or sisters, or father, or mother, or wife, or children, or lands, for my sake, and the gospel's, But he shall receive an hundredfold now in this time, houses, and brethren, and sisters, and mothers, and children, and lands, with persecutions; and in the world to come eternal life. (Mark 10:29-30)

The interesting point is His setting houses and lands in the same connection with kinsfolk: ownership and kinship appear to be lasting relations. Possessions loaned to us for three score and ten years more or less appear in His thought to have their eternal counterparts. He speaks of "true riches" and of something which we can call "our own" as awaiting us in the kingdom of God. Ownership here becomes an education for a similar permanent responsibility.

> If therefore ye have not been faithful in the unrighteous mammon (*the wealth of earth inevitably tainted with imperfect production*

and distribution), who will commit to your trust the true riches? And if ye have not been faithful in that which is another man's (*God's or the community's property*), who shall give you that which is your own? (Luke 16:11-12, additions in italics mine)

CHAPTER FOUR

THE CHRISTIAN AS INVESTOR

IN ANCIENT BABYLON as far back as the days of Hammurabi, about 2200 B.C., we find the system of loaning money at interest; but in the Old Testament there is no trace of commercial credit. The Israelites were an agricultural people, and their trade was mostly in the hands of the Phoenicians and other foreigners. A loan of money was looked on as the sad result of some misfortune — the failure of a crop, a raid by marauders, the pressure of taxation — or as the consequence of extravagant living. The prophets and law-givers hold up lending as a duty of the rich to the poor, but they mean lending without interest.

> If there be among you a poor man of one of thy brethren within any of thy gates in thy land which the Lord thy God giveth thee, thou shalt

> not harden thine heart, nor shut thine hand from thy poor brother: But thou shalt open thine hand wide unto him, and shalt surely lend him sufficient for his need, in that which he wanteth. (Deuteronomy 15:7-8)

Careful provision is made to protect certain kinds of collateral which the borrower may offer. The creditor may not take away a workman's tools, nor keep his heavy cloak over night, nor go into his house to seize his goods. Lending to the poor is praised by psalmists and wise men, while "he that putteth out his money to interest" is classed with liars and slanderers as unfit to enter the Lord's tabernacle (Ps. 15:5).

There are indications, however, that these principles were the ideal held up before the godly, and that they were rarely enforced as statutes of the land. Creditors and debtors are named among the classes in the population, the borrower is spoken of as servant of the lender, and special injunctions are given to prevent creditors selling their fellow-Israelites for debt into slavery. When the Law is taken seriously, its interpreters discovered ways of getting round its provisions against interest. Our Puritan forebears, who regarded the Bible as an infallible rule of practice, as well as of faith, and placed the Old Testament on the same level with the New, managed similarly to shut their eyes to these prohibitions or to explain them away; and they built up our present capitalistic system, which rests upon money loaned at interest. At present the ultra-orthodox will condemn a preacher who does not believe in the historic accuracy of the narrative of some miracle, but one never hears of a heresy trial because a pillar of the church has money in stocks and bonds. Believers in the inerrancy of the Bible are marvelously inconsistent; and in this instance, at least, it is probably wise that they do not press the application of the Biblical text.

But these laws against taking interest applied only to fellow-Israelites: "Thou shalt not lend upon usury to thy brother; usury of money, usury of victuals, usury of any thing that is lent upon usury: Unto a stranger thou mayest lend upon usury" (Deut. 23:19-20). One of the promised blessings of national observance of the Deuteronomic Law was "thou shalt lend unto many nations, but thou shalt not borrow" (Deut. 15:6). Taking interest of one's fellow countrymen and co-religionists was deemed wicked, but outsiders were fair game. Here is another instance of the necessity for Christians of reading even the Bible under the guidance of the Spirit of Christ.

When we turn to the New Testament we find the developed commercial credit system of the Roman world as the background. In the same spirit which moved the prophets and law-givers, Jesus encourages lending: "from him that would borrow of thee turn not thou away" (Matt. 5:42) and "if ye lend to them of whom ye hope to receive, what thank have ye? for sinners also lend to sinners, to receive as much again" (Lk. 6:34). Many of the Church fathers forbade all loaning of money upon interest, basing their teaching on such sayings of Christ and on the passages of the Old Testament. During many Christian centuries a man who loaned money was regarded somewhat as a pawn-broker is looked on among ourselves. The lenders were mostly Jews, whose Law put no obstacles in the way of their lending to Christians, and such usurers were despised, as Shakespeare ridicules Shylock.

In Jesus' parables, however, we see Him accepting the credit system of His day, drawing illustrations from it, and speaking of it without condemnation. He represents the master as saying to the negligent servant: "Thou oughtest therefore to have put my money to the exchangers, and then at my coming I should have received mine own with usury" (Matt. 25:27). But Jesus cannot be quoted as favoring or as forbidding a particular economic system. That is a question He did not consider.

Whatever may be the commercial order of some tomorrow, fifty or a hundred years hence, the world of our time requires capital. Men may differ over questions of its control by the government or by private individuals;

but in any case the government, or a corporation, or an individual, to carry on large enterprises has to borrow capital, and capital is the savings which somebody living or dead has managed to accumulate.

The report of the Federal Reserve Bank for November 1919 gives some startling figures of extravagant buying, and declares that it is not the wage-earners nor those who have possessed wealth for some time who are spending recklessly, but those whose incomes have recently gone up beyond that which is necessary to maintain their former standard of living. Such persons may easily reply to the Bank's strictures that no special class is entitled to luxuries, to wear jewelry and furs, to possess musical instruments and ride in automobiles; and that, if others do, they may, now that they have the price. But as Christians, when a devastated and impoverished world needs capital with which to restore its industries, and when the spread of the kingdom of God both at home and abroad ought to have a much larger financial support, are we not led by the Spirit of Christ to save as much as we can? Some will say: "Let those who have had luxuries for years do the saving, and give those who have never had them the chance." We cannot lay down a rule and define what is luxury. Under existing conditions what seems to one person a bare necessity appears to another a wild extravagance. It is possible that we may some day arrive at more general agreement on these matters of necessary and unnecessary expenditure. For the present it is evident from the experience during the war that many of us can save far more than we usually do. A general wave of saving would lower prices, so helping our poorer brethren, which is a plain Christian duty; would supply us with more to loan for the development of our country's industries and to extend credit to other lands; and would enable us to invest much larger sums in the all-important Christian enterprise of furnishing our land and the world with the convictions and ideals of Jesus, by which we believe international and industrial problems are to be solved, and men, women and children given abundant life. Saving, then, at this moment, for all who possibly can do it, is an unmistakable Christian obligation.

With regard to the investment of our savings what prompting do we receive from the Spirit of Christ? A Christian businessman said recently that years ago he set a certain sum, and made up his mind that, if ever he possessed that much capital, he would make no further income-producing investments, but give away everything that he could save. Here again people will differ widely as to what is the limit of the income-bearing wealth they are justified in retaining. The number of their dependents, their manner of life, their own tastes, are determining factors. Possibly the graduated income-tax may affect men's views on this subject. But ought not many more of our comfortably circumstanced Christians make this businessman's principle theirs? With the perils of great wealth plainly pointed out by our Lord, why should a Christian wish to pile up capital? A useful merchant or professional man need not retire from business because he does not need to make more money. His business or his profession is a service which he should continue to render the community, so long as he has health and strength, unless there be some unremunerative position in which he can be more useful. But let him not go on amassing capital. "Lay not up for yourselves treasures upon earth" (Matt. 6:19). Let him, while he lives, invest as much as he can in distinctively Christian undertakings to serve the physical, the mental and the spiritual needs of men. Does not that seem a principle after the mind of Christ?

With regard to income-producing investments can we discover any leadings of the Spirit? On the porch of a summer club in a group of men a young college graduate let fall the remark that he had taken a flier the previous month in an oil stock, then very active in the market, and had cleared several thousand dollars. A banker who was present asked him abruptly: "What service to the community do you think you performed which entitled you to a sum as large as the salary of many of your hardworking classmates?" Our economists tell us that speculative trading in commodities by experts in them helps to stabilize the market, although Professor Taussig implies that only a small number of such traders are necessary. Men have to be venturesome with their capital as they are with their brains or their labor, if new enterprises are to be undertaken, new inventions developed, new services rendered mankind through commerce and industry.

In addition to Professor Hobhouse's "property for use" and "property for power," named in the last chapter, there is a function for "property for experiment." But taking fliers in stock, as this young man had done, is like gambling with cards or betting on games, a bad thing for the man himself, teaching him to try to get something for nothing, and it also tends to send up the rate of interest on legitimate loans, and so to increase prices, and to place the necessities out of the reach of the poor. The banker's question suggests a Christian principle: "What service to the community do you think you performed by that use of money?" We were urged to invest in Liberty Bonds to help our country in a great cause. Why should Christians make investments for any lower motive? Industries in time of peace render fully as exalted public service as did the army and navy during the war. Should not a Christian satisfy himself that any enterprise — a building, a mine a railway, a factory — into which he puts his savings is fulfilling a necessary ministry to the community, and fulfilling it in a manner that makes for the public welfare? We are followers of One who came to minister, and we wish everything that we control to be serving. We cannot put money into an undertaking simply because it assures large returns; it must approve itself to our consciences as accomplishing a service to the commonwealth.

John Wesley laid down for his followers the three maxims: "Gain all you can; save all you can; give all you can." They have seemed sufficient to many good Christians in the past; but the first maxim hardly satisfies our consciences today. Many persons have felt that in making an investment, all they need think of was the return which they would reap, and that their Christian duty began with the use to which they put their income. But we remember Amos's warning of profiteers who made "the ephah small, and the shekel great" (Amos 8:5). Few here will disagree that we must go further today and assure ourselves that the investment itself performs a service to the community, and a service commensurate with the return on the capital.

Now can we excuse the community through its lawmakers and courts from protecting such investments and seeing that they are employed in the public interest? In some of our large cities down to very recent times there has been a disgraceful abuse of investors by those who managed to get possession of street railway companies. Men and women who put their capital into what was considered a public service corporation possess today in their certificates of stock "scraps of paper;" while our laws have been either so insufficient, or their execution so remissly handled, that the looters of the property have gone to their graves in peace, or still live to build churches with their ill-got gains. While we deplore "reds," let us deal with men who help to produce them. The truest upholders of orderly society are those who set themselves to correct its abuses. Investors must be safe-guarded against financial freebooters, and the community which asks persons to save and invest owes them a reasonable protection.

One sometimes hears men of business use the expression "playing the game," and speak of the fascination of "putting through" some project. Such language may be employed quite harmlessly, but is it safe? Marshaling truth into a sermon and putting it through speech into men's minds has a fascination as an act of skill. Handling a knife and performing a delicate operation is an interesting task to which a surgeon gives himself with zest. But we should shrink from speaking of preaching or operating as fascinating games. One wants to see the ministry of trade and finance on the same level as the ministry of truth and of health. The gusto of a game consists often in beating an opponent; but when this is taken into the sphere of business, in which men's livelihoods are at stake, it becomes a perilous point of view. One wishes that the language of our commercial life could be Christianized. Such adjectives as "cold" and "hard" so frequently applied to a business proposition become hostile to its Christian character; for our God is not a "cold, hard" God, and is ruled out of the control of transactions to which these adjectives are applied. Business should be thought and talked of as a ministry, not as a game. Then what a man receives for his investment in it, in profits or dividends or rent, becomes not his winnings, but his pay; and he will look on it as men did on that which they drew in the service of the country during the war. A right attitude to mind is essential to the creation of a right system: we must Christianize our thought of our relation to business questions before we can see a system in operation that will satisfy our consciences.

And all of us, whether we can save anything or not, have investments to make which will not necessarily bring in any interest in money. Jesus said much of such investments. Over against all uses of capital for the ordinary business of earth which are liable to loss, He urged: "Lay up for yourselves treasures in heaven" (Matt. 6:20). We usually interpret this celestial investment to mean: "Do good things for which you will get little thanks here below, but for which you will receive deferred dividends hereafter." There may be truth in that, but it is hardly our Lord's meaning. We discover what He considered heavenly treasures by looking at the things in which He was Himself wealthy. There was His power of appreciation — appreciation of grass of the field and the play of children in the market-place; appreciation of people — Simon Peter, John, Nathanael, the young ruler, Zacchaeus, and the rest of the figures who live on the Gospel pages; appreciation of God. Appreciativeness pays huge dividends: and it both yields an unfailing income and is ever increasing its capital. There was His ability to get on with people— His consideration, tact, patience, friendliness — these enrich a man in his contacts with his fellows and help him to get on with his Father in heaven, to be "rich toward God." There was His skill in doing for people which made Him so valuable an addition to any circle or town, any home or synagogue, in which He was, and would enable Him to bring untold wealth to the city of God. Learning to appreciate, to get on with others, to be skilled in doing for them — these are ways of laying up treasure in heaven, methods of accumulating capital which will never pass its dividends here or in any other part of God's universe.

The Church as the Body of Christ is the incorporation

of a number of His disciples investing together their wealth of appreciation, of fellowship, of skill in serving their community and world. Unfortunately the membership roll of most churches contains the names of many who make no investment. An owner of a chicken farm in Connecticut recently had one of the experts in the state's employ visit his farm. Prior to the expert's coming a careful record had been kept of the eggs laid daily in each house. The expert looked the hens over and put aside sixty *per cent* as slackers. In the weeks that followed the record showed that the remaining forty *per cent* produced ninety-five *per cent* of the eggs, while the sixty *per cent* of the hens contributed only five *per cent.* In most churches there is a similar proportion of workers and slackers, and the slackers are by no means exclusively or predominantly among the ecclesiastical hens. A farmer can order his unprofitable chickens to instant execution; but a church's problem with its unproductive members is more difficult of solution.

Jesus definitely connects the investment of money with heavenly wealth: "Make to yourselves friends of the mammon of unrighteousness" (Lk. 16:9). He would have us turn our savings in money into relationships with people. A business which is carried on as a service of men's needs, or a loan made to an impoverished nation to set its industries on their feet, fulfills that requirement.

Such an investment of capital sets mills going, carries people and goods where they need to be taken, supplies food, affords pleasure. Would that we could see the text applied to every dollar invested in bonds or placed in a savings bank! To substitute the friendly hand for the grasping hand in the use of capital is to Christianize its investment. Paul was speaking of the use of money when he spoke of sowing to the Spirit.

And Jesus' saying about making friends out of money suggests, more particularly, friendly approaches to men from which we expect no financial return. The support of hospitals, of schools, of churches, are all friendly services. And as Christians we need to think carefully of the levels on which we wish to try to be friends. All kindly people, whatever their beliefs, want to befriend men in physical want, and Christians will do their share in this. All intelligent people, whatever their creed, want to befriend the mental needs of mankind; and Christians will do their full part in the work of education. But today when we have had brought home to us through the terrors of war that healthy bodies and highly trained minds may belong to beastly men, that nations may have abundance for the physical and intellectual necessities of their people and leave them spiritually paupers, Christians will want above all things to befriend men's spirits. In view of the capital that is in Christian hands, the enterprise of pushing the kingdom of Christ ought to have a vastly larger investment. This is to turn money into the highest form of friendliness, the friendship of men in Christ.

And Jesus gives His reason for urging this transmutation of wealth from possession of things, which can exist for us here only, into contacts with people who will be with us forever: "And I say unto you, Make to yourselves friends of the mammon of unrighteousness; that, when ye fail, they may receive you into everlasting habitation" (Lk. 16:9). Whatever such dwellings may be, it will be friendly people who will make them homelike for you and me. What a prospect of entering on a fellowship with persons, many of whom we have never seen, but with whom we begin on the basis of friendship in the eternal kingdom, because we invested ourselves and our means in undertakings which enriched them with the friendship of Christ, the mutual Friend of us all!

CHAPTER FIVE

THE CHRISTIAN AS EMPLOYER AND EMPLOYEE

THE OLD TESTAMENT has little to say upon employer and employed because throughout a large part of Israel's history it was not a common relation. The word translated "servant" usually means "slave" and the bondman like a wife or an ox or an ass, was considered his master's property. War and want were the two chief sources of slaves. A successful military leader, such as Joshua or David, made captives who served as the drudges of their victors, their hewers of fire-wood and drawers of water. The failure of a crop or some other calamity might reduce a small farmer to debt, and compel him to sell himself and his family to a wealthier neighbor who could maintain them. It was against this bondage for debt that Amos protested, when he spoke of the needy as sold for a paltry sum, the price of a pair of shoes. The Hebrews could not forget that they had themselves been slaves in Egypt, and in the midst of a world where slavery was universal their legislation attempted to assure an enslaved Hebrew his social and his religious rights; and it also threw some humane safeguards about the enslaved foreigner.

The later law-givers undertook to prohibit altogether the holding of fellow-Israelites, and to permit only the possession of slaves belonging to other nations:

> And if thy brother that dwelleth by thee be waxen poor, and be sold unto thee; thou shalt not compel him to serve as a bondservant: But as an hired servant, and as a sojourner, he shall be with thee, and shall serve thee unto the year of jubile. And then shall he depart from thee, both he and his children with him, and shall return unto his own family, and unto the possession of his fathers shall he return. (Leviticus 25:39-41)

And,

> Both thy bondmen, and thy bondmaids, which thou shalt have, shall be of the heathen that are round about you; of them shall ye buy bondmen and bondmaids. (Leviticus 25:44)

Hired servants are occasionally mentioned; but the

only specific provision for them in the Law decrees the prompt payment of their wages:

> Thou shalt not oppress an hired servant that is poor and needy, whether he be of thy brethren, or of thy strangers that are in thy land within thy gates: At his day thou shalt give him his hire, neither shall the sun go down upon it; for he is poor, and setteth his heart upon it: lest he cry against thee unto the Lord, and it be sin unto thee. (Deuteronomy 24:14-15)

We may sum up the Old Testament's teaching as a plea for humaneness.

In the New Testament also "servant" remains usually a translation for "slave;" and the background is the more degraded position of the bondman in Greco-Roman society. In Palestine slaves seem not to have been more than a fraction of the population. When the exiles returned under Nehemiah, the figures are some forty-two thousand free-men to about seven thousand slaves: a ratio of six to one. But in the Athens of the corresponding date it is estimated that there were four slaves to every citizen. In the little island of Aegina, slightly less than twice the size of Manhattan in extent, there were at one period 470,000 slaves. Wealthy Roman land-owners are said to have possessed as many as ten or twenty thousand on their estates. The slave was at his master's disposal: he had no rights of marriage; and for the smallest offense he might be scourged, mutilated, crucified, or thrown to the wild beasts. It is a well known fact that wherever slaves are common, free labor has a low position; and the hireling is not esteemed when he is mentioned in the New Testament: "The hireling fleeth, because he is an hireling, and careth not for the sheep" (Jn. 10:13).

Jesus was familiar with slavery in its milder Palestinian form; but in one of His parables He alludes to the power of the master to punish a bondman: "The lord of that servant shall come in a day when he looketh not for him, and in an hour that he is not aware of, And shall cut him asunder" (Matt. 24:50-51). And in another parable He speaks of a master delivering his slave to the tormenters. He gives no specific teaching as to slavery, and it is doubtful whether He judged the institution one way or another; but He proclaims the brotherhood of all men as God's children. He refers occasionally to hired servants; and His own feelings may be caught in that suggestive parable where a proprietor seeking laborers finds the unemployed in the market-place, and with a conscience for the living wage gives those who work only a fraction of the day a full day's pay. But Jesus does not treat of the relation of employer and employed. He inculcates the spirit of service and of brotherhood, and leaves men to apply it.

Paul encountered the severer slavery of the Greco-Roman world. It is unlikely that he ever considered the moral basis of the institution; that was not a question in his time. He sends back the runaway, Onesimus, and, like Jesus, he bids Philemon treat him as "a brother beloved" (Philem. 1:16). He advised bondmen who could obtain their freedom to avail themselves of the chance: "if thou mayest be made free, use it rather" (1 Cor. 7:21) and he warned Christians against falling into the *status* of slaves: "Ye are bought with a price; be not ye the servants of men" (1 Cor. 7:23). He insisted that in Christ there could not be bond and free; and so he did away, at least as between Christians, with the servile relation of property to owner. Jesus and His apostles were not revolutionists, in the sense of assaulting a particular social system; but they were radicals, who put leaven into society that was destined to work a complete transformation.

Three centuries after Paul, we find a Christian preacher, John Chrysostom, telling his hearers that, if they really care for their slaves, they must "buy them, and having taught them some art that they may maintain themselves, set them free." "I know," he adds, as a preacher of today occasionally feels when discussing industrial questions, "I know that I am annoying my hearers; but what can

I do? For this purpose I am appointed, and I will not cease speaking so." The total effect of Christianity upon relations which seem to imply superiority and inferiority was well expressed in a book written by Goldwin Smith in 1863, when the slavery struggle was still on in this country: "The brotherhood of man is the idea which Christianity in its social phase has been always striving to realize, and the progress of which constitutes the social history of Christendom. With what difficulties this idea has struggled; how it has been marred by revolutionary violence, as well as impeded by reactionary selfishness; to what chimerical hopes, to what wild schemes, to what calamitous disappointments, to what desperate conflicts, it has given birth; how often being misunderstood and misapplied, it has brought not peace on earth but a sword — it is needless here to rehearse. Still, as we look back over the range of past history, we can see beyond doubt that it is towards this goal that Christianity as a social principle has been always tending and still tends."

In applying Christian principles to the relationships of employers and employed in our time, it is convenient to distinguish between personal relations, such as a farmer has with his help, a housekeeper with domestics, or a businessman with his secretary or office-boy, and the more impersonal relations of wage-earners and employers in industrial enterprises.

In the personal contacts of employer and employed sincere Christians have found it possible to embody the Spirit of Christ in both positions. They have lived together in these relations in mutual respect, confidence and affection. That seems to be the correct order in which these nouns should be placed. Let employer and employed learn first to respect each other, then to trust and be worthy of each other's trust, and brotherly love follows. In this country the use of the words "master" and "mistress" in this connection is practically obsolete, save in real estate parlance, where the phrase "master's bedrooms" remains current; but that is merely a convenient designation, and the housing accommodations of those in service have markedly improved within a generation. Among us no Christian employer feels justified in asking for an attitude of deferential servility — that is recognized as both unamerican and unchristian. An employer's main obligation can be summed up in the words "considerate justice." He must be thoughtful of an employee's leisure, a leisure that may be fairly counted on and is not subject to sudden change or interruption; thoughtful of his independence, so that he does not intermeddle with private matters nor attempt, however benevolently, to play providence and arrange another's affairs; thoughtful of his employee's social and spiritual opportunities. Certain positions appear to doom those who fill them to needless loneliness and reduce them to mental starvation. And even nominally Christian employers are shamefully unregarding of the spirits of those who serve them. A woman in domestic employment in bringing her church letter said that the employer in whose household she lived had the impression that she was a Roman Catholic, "and" she said, "please do not let her know that I'm not; because when they think you a Roman Catholic, they feel that you *must* be let off to attend church, and will even help to get you there; while, if you're a Protestant, it doesn't much matter."

And "considerate justice" may equally sum up the duties of the employee in these personal relations. It is a great shame that certain customs such as the receiving of commissions on purchases, occasional pilfering, and the taking of tips, tend to lower the dignity of some employments. These are practices which should be abolished by common Christian consent. Both positions of employer and employed have been used by tactful and earnest Christians as opportunities to exert an influence for Christ. One might suppose that an employer had more advantages in this matter; but in experience one discovers employees even more conscientious in drawing their employers, and particularly their employers' children, to the friendship of Christ.

It is in the largely impersonal relations of modem

industry that we have been less successful in embodying Christian brotherhood. The impersonal character of the relations is responsible for much. A New England manufacturer who served on the War Labor Board ascribes eighty *per cent* of the difficulties between employers and employed which came under his observation to absentee management. The more remote a member of the employing group is from the laborer, the less likely is he to appreciate his point of view. But this is not the entire difficulty. No one can be content with the present situation in which employers and employed are drawn up in mutually suspicious and hostile camps, and the community suffers from an epidemic of wasteful and embittering strikes and lockouts, calling often for the armed intervention of police and troops. Thoughtful men realize that the existing state of affairs cannot be indefinitely prolonged. Some cataclysm will occur, and by this time, God knows, we ought to appreciate what cataclysms mean. As Christians we are confident that we possess the secret of avoiding such a disaster; we know that the situation can be entirely changed if we can induce men to adopt our spiritual principle. We look on society as a living organism, and believe that social systems have to be grown, not made; so we are not advocating some ready-made scheme of industrial reorganization. We are eager for the intelligent and hearty adoption of the Christian point of view. We know how slavery was immediately altered and ultimately abolished when men accepted Christian brotherhood. We are convinced that once the Christian mind dominates our industrial situation, methods of Christian adjustment will follow. We, therefore, try to face present conditions with the searching conscience of Christ.

A first criticism of ourselves is with our attitude both as employers and employees towards the public; we are too generally competing for private gain instead of co-operating for public service. There was a time, and that not so remote, when the attitude of those in control of some of our large corporations was expressed in the graphic phrase: "The public be damned!" Today a similar attitude is occasionally taken by the leaders of a powerful labor union. We have to remind both that from the Christian standpoint they are fellow-servants of the community. And we cannot fail to be sympathetic with efforts made by the community to assert its right to be served, and to insist that employers and employed concern themselves primarily with meeting its needs, looking only for a compensation which the community considers a reasonable return for the services they render. A city's milk supply cannot be left to the milk companies and their employees; both may combine to exploit the public. We have for some years protected the city's health by rules regarding the production and delivery of milk. We are evidently going further, and inquiring what are the costs of milk, and what are fair compensations for those who participate in the industry — compensations that offer sufficient inducements to procure the supply which we need. Such determinations are difficult and delicate. Public service commissions may be unintelligent and even unjust. But the trend of the day is towards some form of social control of essential industries. It is a further development of democracy; and, as Christians, we cannot do other than sympathize with it, because it asserts and attempts to embody our fundamental principle that all who take part in industry are servants of the commonwealth. We do not allow soldiers or policemen to strike; their loyalty to the community demands that they fulfill their functions.

But have not those who are charged with the ministry of necessary industries, be they owners of mines or of sugar plantations, or employees in any vital public service, a similar responsibility? Must we not remind them that they, too, have a civic duty? To be sure we must guarantee to them proper means of airing grievances and righting wrongs. We must grant them the right to resign from their positions, as we allow public servants to give up their posts. No man can be compelled to work. But the community's right to be served must be paramount in a Christian society. We have a great deal of machinery to develop and set in operation to make this effective, but the Christian principle involved seems clear as day. We tell ourselves as employers and employed in all the essential ministries of transportation, of fuel, of food, of clothing, of health, of education, of religion, that we are fellow-servants of the community and must work together in its service.

Our next criticism has to do with the relation of employers and employed to each other. Hitherto the employee has been usually looked on as a "hand," rather than as a citizen of industry. His labor has been viewed as a commodity to be sold in the "labor market." His work has been more considered than his personality. If it were more profitable to employ him casually, he was taken on and laid off, regardless of the ill effects casual employment has in producing casual character. He has had no voice in the enterprise in which he served. The employer has been given autocratic control of industry, so far as his employees were concerned. It may have made for efficiency in material organization; it has not promoted brotherhood in the relations of man and man.

And it is plain that this, too, is rapidly passing. Labor has organized to protect its interests. The combination of wage-earners in unions for collective bargaining is justified, like universal military training, by the necessities of a time of strife. The two systems are closely akin. Both organize men for defense; both stress loyalty to the group; both tend to subordinate the individual's freedom and conscience to the group's will. Both claim many incidental advantages for those whom they thus organize — training in common action, in self-sacrifice, in devotion to a cause. Both lay stress upon discipline — conformity to rules. But from a Christian point of view both have the grave defect of being organizations for conflict. They stimulate the combative and not the creative spirit. We should not have a more Christian adjustment of our industries, if all employers were combined on one side, in their organizations, and all employees on the other side in their unions, any more than we should have more Christian international relations did all nations drill every able-bodied male inhabitant in their populations.

Recently both in Britain and in this country a number of organizations have sprung up, known as Works Councils, or by some similar title, which try to combine employers and employed in a given enterprise in a common attempt to increase the efficiency of their business, to settle differences, to foster goodwill, and to give all concerned a voice in the control and a sense of responsibility for the success of their industry. The forms of organization vary; the extent to which employees participate in control differs. The movement is as yet in its infancy, and the results are still too meager to make a sound judgment on the plan possible. Like all methods, its success depends upon the spirit in which it is conceived and attempted. If it be a pretense at brotherhood, it is foredoomed. But in less than two years this scheme, which is widely used in Britain, has been adopted by more than two hundred establishments in this country employing half a million workers. It seems a congenial method of advance for the Christian spirit.

And it is of vital moment that we Christians exercise our ministry of reconciliation in our industries today. The radical would do away with the employer and place the employees in complete control, but industry requires trained leadership. The conservative would maintain efficiency by keeping the control exclusively in the employer's power; but production requires the hearty goodwill of the employees, and that is notoriously lacking. As followers of Jesus we believe in fellowship, in bringing representatives of seemingly hostile interests face to face, and keeping them in personal contact, in getting them to share responsibilities and to lose their selfishness in the more inclusive aim of the community's service.

And this brings us to our most serious quarrel with things as they are — the assumption that every man, employer or employee, can be moved only by his self-interest. When the Constitutional Convention was discussing the question of allowing slavery in the new Republic, John Rutledge of South Carolina said: "Religion and humanity have nothing to do with this question. Interest alone is the governing principle with nations. The true question is whether the Southern States shall or shall not be parties to the union." When religion and humanity are subordinated to self-interest, an economic and industrial catastrophe is prepared for, as happened in the Civil War; and the disaster was severest for those whose forebears chose the path of self-interest. Any scheme which appeals mainly to this incentive is doomed to a similar tragic judgment. We cannot build a golden society out of leaden motives. We did not appeal to self-interest when we asked men to hazard their lives for the world's freedom, and they responded gloriously to a far loftier appeal. We must plead for their consecration to render our industries worthy of the day of brotherhood for which many of the soldier-dead wistfully dreamed. The parable of Jesus in which laborers receive the same pay for longer and shorter days expressly teaches that what a man gets is not to be his incentive to work. Paul wisely told both slaves and freemen to abide in their callings "with God." This means that both employers and employed seek first to share the point of view and the motives of the Father of Jesus Christ. With such outlooks and aims, agreements can be reached; for persons who seem to touch nowhere else can find themselves in contact in the love of God. And despite all cynical remarks about human nature, is it not true that by and large employers and employed today really wish to end the straining, embittering, warlike reign of self-seeking, and to substitute the reign of devoted service?

They may not phrase it in that language; but is not every chamber of commerce and employers' association, and every workingmen's union, sincerely eager to have done with the present era of selfish strife? Here is the Church's chance to interpret to men their own desires, to point out that whatever they think they want — and they may be thinking largely in terms of material good things for themselves and theirs — they really want to serve in brotherhood, and that this alone would satisfy them and make possible the attainment of other things which are always added to those who seek first to serve in fellowship. Here is our chance to hold up before them and before ourselves God as willing this better day, willing it just as soon as we are willing to let Him give it to us, for a day of the Lord is always "at hand." Here is our chance to reassert our Christian faith in men — in captains of industry and in the lowliest privates in the ranks — as capable of working in the trades and commerce of today, as did the Carpenter of Nazareth, and of forming together one comradeship of labor, as the mind which was in

Christ is formed in us.

And before we leave this subject it is worth noting that the writers of the New Testament, who so constantly stress brotherhood between man and man, when they think of their relation to Jesus, do not call themselves His brethren, although they think He so calls them; nor do they regard themselves as his hired servants, as though they were free to leave him at will. With all their newly awakened manhood, they subscribe themselves "slaves of Jesus Christ." They give themselves to Him completely and forever. They wish to be owned by Him outright. While with one another and with all men they are brethren, One is their Master, even Christ.

CONCLUSION

DEMOCRACY AND FAITH

THE MOVEMENT in the industrial world of our day is often described as a demand for industrial democracy. The phrase needs to be defined. It is evidently employed in widely differing senses by President Wilson and Bill Haywood, a leader of the Industrial Workers of the World. It has been used as the subtitle of a book, in which the writer describes a limited participation of factory operatives in the control of the conditions of their work and in the share of half of a certain arbitrarily calculated increased profit. But there are three factors at present in industry — the investors, the workers, and the consumers — and we cannot label "industrial democracy" any form of organization in which all three are not represented and in which the determining factor is not the public — the community whom the industry serves.

Democracy is not a distinctively Christian product,

although Christianity has probably been the most potent single force in developing it; but it is so congruous with the Spirit of Christ that today Christians cannot do otherwise than sympathize with its political and industrial advances. And democracy makes a vast demand upon faith — faith in the capacities of ordinary men and women, faith in the power of spiritual ideals, faith in the universe as friendly to brotherhood.

Faith in the capacities of ordinary men and women. Those who oppose allowing the workers a voice in the management of a factory or a mine are wont to say: "Do you suppose that unskilled laborers, or even fairly skilled laborers, are fit to share in running this enterprise?" On the other hand radicals assert that the present capitalists are not worthy to be entrusted with any control in the railroads or mills of the system which they hope to inaugurate. Both sides approach the subject with a want of faith in man.

Wars have usually been followed by reactionary periods in which counsels of timidity and distrust have prevailed and there has been a tendency to concentrate authority in a few strong hands. After the Wars of the Roses came the Tudors; after the civil strife of the Commonwealth era the Stuarts were restored; after the Napoleonic epoch the Bourbons returned. In 1812 we find Walter Scott writing to Robert Southey in words that sound strangely familiar at this moment:

> You are quite right in apprehending a *Jacquerie*: the country is mined below our feet. Last week, learning that a meeting was to be held among the weavers of a large manufacturing village of Galashiels, for the purpose of cutting a man's web from his loom, I apprehended the ringleaders and disconcerted the project; but in the course of my inquiries, imagine my surprise at discovering a bundle of letters and printed manifestoes, from which it appeared that the Manchester Weavers' Committee corresponds with every manufacturing town in the South and West of Scotland and levies a subsidy of 2s.6d. per man — (an immense sum) — for the ostensible purpose of petitioning Parliament for redress of grievances, but doubtless to sustain them in their revolutionary movements. An energetic administration would soon check all this; but it is sickening to think of our situation.

But we recall the pitiable plight of the weavers at that time when power-looms were being introduced, and know that Scott's Tory feelings, intensified by his military training in the local militia, which had been organized to ward off a feared attack by Napoleon on Britain, led him to cruel distrust of his fellow-countrymen.

It is easy to run down the mass of human beings. Millions are woefully ignorant; millions more are lazy; most are hideously selfish. The war revealed abysmal depths in Germans and Turks, and race riots have shown no less brutality in some white Americans. It is perilous to have a blind confidence in people — to expect uneducated negroes to show the same self-control as long-civilized Anglo-Saxons, to anticipate the operatives of a factory to be suddenly gifted with business skill to assume its direction, to fancy Chinese coolies and Russian peasants in a twinkling competent for self-government, to think a labor-union less selfish than the stockholders of a corporation. But it is even more perilous to trust people too little — to believe that negroes must remain moral and mental inferiors to be cowed by violence, that workers cannot be developed to share business responsibilities, that Chinese or Koreans or Hindus are incapable of being trained to self-government, that both stockholders and workers cannot be inspired with the motives of public service. With such unbelief we shall fall back on a creed, like Nietzsche's, that a few supermen ought to be allowed by their shrewdness and force to inherit the earth and impose their will on the herd of common folk. But how are we to gain this faith in the capacities of ordinary men and women, the creative faith which awakens in them that which they are trusted to be? That is our first problem.

A second faith which an enthusiast for democracy requires is *belief in the power of spiritual ideals.* It is supposed that self-interest is the only motive strong enough to drive men to fight or to work or to do any of life's difficult and monotonous things. Many insist upon looking at labor disputes as quarrels over money only; and the notion that a workman wishes to be a citizen of industry and to be recognized as a partner is far above out of their sight. It is the same frame of mind which insists on viewing the settlement of the Peace solely from the angle of national interest.

Those were timely lines which Alfred Noyes penned last summer:

> Now in this morning of a nobler age,
>   Though night-born eyes, long taught to fear the sun,
> Would still delay the world's great heritage,
>   Make firm, O God, the peace our dead have won,
> For folly shakes the tinsel on her head
>   And points us back to darkness and to hell,
> Cackling — "Beware of visions," while our dead
>   Still cry, "It was for visions that we fell."

No democracy, either in war or in peace, can dispense with the stimulus of vision. And the extension of democracy to industry presupposes responsiveness to the claims of the community, consecration to the service of the commonwealth, consciences sensitive to the appeals of brotherhood. Many frankly have no confidence in the potency of altruistic ideals. How are we to steady our own faith and render it contagious? That is our second problem.

A third faith which the devotee of democracy must possess is *belief in the universe as friendly to this fraternal order*. One is amazed at the naïve confidence of many socially minded persons who are so sure that a juster and kindlier industrial order is possible, without troubling to ask themselves whether the world in which we live is meant for a human brotherhood. The fabric of nature seems constructed along contrary lines. The race is to the swift and the battle to the strong. Wars rage everywhere among germs, plants, insects, fish, beasts, and have always been waged by men. The advocates of social progress have often found nature a stumbling-block. "The whole subject of the brute creation," wrote Dr. Thomas Arnold, "is to me one of such painful mystery that I dare not approach it." And scientists hardly increase our faith by their predictions of what is to be. In 1909 M. J. de Morgan, a leading French anthropologist, wrote:

The glacial period is far from being ended; our

> times which still make an integral part of it, are characterized by an important retreat of the glaciers, started long before the beginnings of history. It is to be supposed that this retreat of the ice is not definitive, but that the cold will return, and with it the depopulation of a part of our globe. Nothing can enable us to foretell the amplitude of this future oscillation, or the lot which the laws of nature destine to humanity. During this cataclysm revolutions will occur which the most fecund imagination cannot conceive — disasters the more horrible because, while the population of the earth goes on increasing every day, and even the less favored districts become little by little inhabited, the different groups, crowded back one on another and finding no more space for existence, will be driven to internecine destruction.

That is hardly a prospect calculated to confirm our hope of the progress of brotherhood. Milton makes his Eve, the day after the first tragedy in Eden, say to Adam:

> See, the morn,
> All unconcern'd with our unrest, begins
> Her rosy progress smiling.

What assurance have we that this earth, in which we are both children and aliens, is the ally of our hopes, is meant for a democratic society of friendly nations and an industrial order of brethren laboring together in mutual trust and service? That is our third problem.

The supreme contribution which Christians have to offer is the religious solution of these three problems. Our historic faith in God corresponds to democracy's threefold need for faith — faith in the capacities of plain people, faith in the power of spiritual ideals, faith in the universe as friendly to brotherhood. We believe in God revealed in a plain Man, the Carpenter of Nazareth; in God the Holy Spirit present in all ideals akin to those of this Man; in God the Father, Lord of heaven and earth, assuring the alliance of the entire creation with such ideals and guaranteeing their victory. A more Christian industrial order can come only as the answer to a larger confidence in the God and Father of Jesus Christ. According to our faith it is done unto us.

We believe in the capacities of ordinary men and women because we have seen what a man can be in Jesus, the Son of God. If one child of the Father's, made in all points like unto His brethren, can as a workman at his bench and as a teacher with his pupils contain the fullness of the Godhead, can be governed by the love and disclose the wisdom of the Lord of the universe, every child of

God is equally capacious. Jesus lived in a subject people, with no more voice in its government than a Korean in the Japanese Empire or a negro in some of our southern states. What a loss to the Syria of the First Century and to the Roman Empire that a conscience and mind like His had no chance to be felt directly in public policies!

When an autocratic employer asks: "Are the operatives in this mill fit to share in its management?" we must probably answer: "Not wholly; nor, for that matter, are you entirely fit. But both you and they have capacities as children of God, which must be developed by the chance to put conscience and heart in a fellowship of service. Who knows what enrichment to this enterprise, to you and to them, will follow the sense that the business is your joint ministry to the commonwealth?" We believe in the capacities of men, not because of what we see in them at present, but because of what we have seen in our Kinsman, the Son of man, and because in trusting in one another, as He trusted us, we can evoke the human nature which He brings out.

We believe in the power of Christlike ideals — ideals of justice, of service, of brotherhood — not because we see these triumphing all about us. Viewed across long stretches of history it is manifest that they do conquer. The union or the corporation which sets itself to thwart justice is doomed. The nation which violates brotherhood will reap a ghastly harvest. The man who snaps his fingers at the obligations of public service will find himself an impoverished soul. But these results take time in which to show themselves; and there are periods in which ideals appear to lose their force. Bishop Gore said recently:

> There is now the usual depression and lowering of moral aims which always follows a time of war. For the real terror of war is not during the struggle; then the war has very ennobling powers. It is the after-war periods which are the curse of the world, and it looks as though this were going to prove true today. I own that I never felt anxiety such as I do now. I think the aspect of things has never been quite so dark as at this moment. I think the temper of the nations has degraded since the Armistice to a degree that is almost terrifying.

But our faith in the potency of spiritual ideals rests in our conviction that things are no mere aspirations of high-minded men and women; they are inspirations from the Most Highest; they are the Spirit of God in man. The restlessness of our day is partly earth-born — the selfish striving for the possession of things, that "covetousness, which is idolatry;" (Col. 3:5) partly it is the breath of heaven, stirring our consciences to a more just distribution both of the burdens and of the satisfactions of life, to a more considerate arrangement of our methods of work and enjoyment, so that the whole family of mankind, severally and collectively, receive their Father's bounteous provision for their bodies, minds and spirits.

Lincoln, the most conspicuous exponent of the democratic ideal, wrote to his friend, Joshua Speed: "I have no doubt it is the peculiar misfortune of both you and me to dream dreams of Elysium far exceeding all that anything earthly can realize." "*Peculiar misfortune*?" — they were his power by which the union was conserved and the slave set free. The Christlike ideals which haunt us in this day of international reorganization and industrial readjustment — however scoffed at as chimerical — are to us promptings of the All-wise, which we may calmly, courageously and confidently espouse.

And we believe that the universe is friendly to the brotherly scheme of things, not because nature looks differently to us than to other men. Who of us is not time and again baffled and overcome by the inexplicable in the structure of the earth we know, by the sufferings of human beings, by the dark mysteries which leave us saying with our wisest Guide: "My God, why?" (Mk. 15:34). In every age the world, as men view it, has been a cross to faith. But followers of Jesus reach up into the unseen and lay hold of One like Him, His Father, and tell themselves that He is God. It is not a pure assumption; we pile up corroborative evidence. We try to make this brute universe answer the needs of men and we discover that it responds to our mastery. We turn deserts into gardens by irrigation; we make an acre yield a larger crop by scientific agriculture; we breed better horses and cattle; we conquer many diseases or render ourselves immune against their attacks; we convert pestilential regions into healthy dwelling-places; we satisfy the wants of many more men as the result of inventions. And this requires cooperation — brother leagued with brother. If the dwellings on one block are left unsanitary, tuberculosis, starting there, menaces an entire city. Our plague of Influenza is thought to have originated in North China, so that hospitals and physicians sent to mission fields may be no small factor in safeguarding health in home lands. Every man's invention is a trust which he dare not keep for his private use. All progress is due to team-work, the chemist assisting the pathologist, the student in the laboratory the farmer in the field, the scientist the manufacturer. It is man's collective approach to which nature responds. But it remains an act of faith on our part to fancy that the universe is designed to serve and befriend us, and that to our fellowship in study and toil it will yield a gracious answer. That faith rests in a fatherly God, who made and rules it for the good of the family of

His children.

On the eastern border of California amid the high Sierras above the Nevada desert lies a deep lake. For ages it has been there, waiting with its life-giving water to befriend the arid plain below. Some years since its waters were carried down through a tunnel and a canal, and sent out over the dry waste through irrigating ditches. And today the former desert is green with alfalfa and trees and gardens. That fructifying water on the heights, coming through these opened approaches, showing its presence in the fruitful plain is a symbol of the Christian God "over all, and through all, and in all," (Eph. 4:6) — Father, Son, and Holy Spirit.

It is a happy augury for the Christian Church that men are resolving to seek a more fraternal industrial order. We can heartily sympathize with their endeavor. We must spiritualize their desires, lifting them from things as ends, to things as means to mutual service. We must use the Spirit of Christ to point out the next steps to be taken by us as producers and consumers, owners and investors, employers and employees. We shall find in the unconscious faith of our time a predisposition to the historic faith of the Church, and we can fortify men's resolve and establish their confidence by proclaiming God — the God whom they want, and the God who to those who trust Him assures the coming of the more Christian industrial order of our passionate hope.

SCRIPTURE INDEX

About The Greater Heritage

Mission

The Greater Heritage is a Christian publishing ministry that equips believers for an abundant life of service, personal spiritual growth and character development.

What We Do

The Greater Heritage publishes original articles, books, Bible studies and church resources. All of its books are made entirely in the USA.

Want to publish with us? Inquire at:

The Greater Heritage
1170 Tree Swallow Dr., Suite 309
Winter Springs, Florida 32708
info@thegreaterheritage.com
www.thegreaterheritage.com

Find more books and our latest catalog online at:

www.thegreaterheritage.com/shop

THE Greater Heritage
Christian Publishing

SPREAD THE WORD - SHARE THIS BOOK

If you enjoyed this book, please consider sharing it with others. There are many ways to share, including...

- Take a **photo** with the book and post it on your social media page(s).
- Write a **review** on your blog or on an online store's product page.
- Share a **copy** with friends and family or buy one as a gift.
- Recommend this book to your circle of influence.
- Follow The Greater Heritage on Twitter: **@TGH_Ministries**.
- Subscribe to our email list at www.thegreaterheritage.com.

CPSIA information can be obtained
at www.ICGtesting.com
Printed in the USA
BVHW031456100323
660174BV00013B/873

9 781953 855350